The Heart of the
Rose

By Mabel A. McKee

Layout and Cover Copyright ©2010
All Rights Reserved
Printed in the USA

Published by ReadaClassic.com
ISBN#: 9781611043518

Table of Contents

The Heart of the Rose 4

The Heart of the Rose

He was her brother. The thought gave her the same thrill this morning as it had given her on a morning seventeen years back, when the old family doctor had laid a tiny bundle in her arms and said, "You'll have to be his sister and mother both, Elizabeth."

Her twelve years then hung heavily on her; her little face, stained with the marks of recent tears, took on a warmer glow as she touched the baby's hand. She had unfolded the baby blanket and slipped on his first little clothes. And as she dressed him, she felt a sense of loss; with every fresh garment he seemed to become less of an angel and more of a human being. The same feeling of loss was now in her heart as she folded his great Indian blankets, slipped his photographs into the case and filled the nooks and crevices of his trunk with "little surprises" to drive away the first bitter longings for home. She lifted a thick white wool sweater; it brought the memory of a little soft flannel shirt. She buried her face in its folds and murmured in a tearful voice, "Why, he is my man brother and I am sending him from home to college."

* * * * *

His foot sounded on the stairway; his clear boyish voice called, "Beth, where are you?"

Before she could answer he entered the room. Throwing several bundles onto the bed, he gave a sigh of relief. He tugged impatiently at the strings as he explained: "These are some things the girls made me. It's great to be going away, isn't it? Why, I feel just like I was getting out of a cage; I feel like I was going to fly. Say, what is this, anyway?"

He held up a small book, shaped to resemble the bud of a flower. It was made of white water-color paper and every leaf was fastened to the other leaves by small white cords. On the front was the picture of a baby; on the back was a pair of black kid doll shoes.

"Where did you get it?" his sister asked.

"Rose gave it to me; she told me a long time ago that she was making me a book of memories; that I was to open just one page a week. That's my baby picture, all right, but why on earth has she put those doll slippers on the back? And why is it shaped in this funny way? What makes girls such strange creatures, anyway, Beth?"

She laughed. "I guess, Floyd, if this is a book of memories, that last page is to picture the last great event of your life—your graduation night. Don't you remember how your new patent leathers pinched your feet, so that you limped across the platform after your diploma? It is shaped like a rosebud, for it is like that. Every week you will open a new petal, and finally, when you have opened them all, it will be a full-blown rose. When you come back Rose will have unfolded a few petals, too."

"Well, I am going to unfold every one of these right now. I never could wait that long to see what is in the center. Of course I have a vague idea, but I want to be sure. So in two minutes we will know this mystery."

"No," she said firmly, taking the book from his hand. "What

would the book mean to you then, Floyd? Every particle of the pleasure—the expectation—would be gone. It took Rose a long time to make this book and you surely would not destroy its value in a few minutes. She even formed every leaf like a petal, so that it would give you the pleasure of watching it unfold like a real rose. It is just a symbol of herself—a little bud of promise."

"She's great to think of all that; I like her. Oh, she and Dorothy are going to stop a minute tonight; Dot has something for me and I want them to see some of my things. But I do want to open this book. I guess I will give it to you to keep until I am ready to shut this trunk, so it won't be such a temptation. But let's eat pretty soon; I am simply starved."

At the supper table he talked incessantly of his departure. One moment he wished that she could go along; the next he exulted over the idea of being in a house with a crowd of fellows. While he talked a boy came to the door and was dragged in by a ruthless hand. While they ate quantities of hot waffles they talked of the "fellows and girls." For the most part they talked of the girls. The sister heard new phrases—a new language; he had always used a different one to her. They spoke of girls as "four-flushers," as "easies," as "stiffs" and "stand-patters." Occasionally Floyd stopped in the center of a remark and nodded his head warningly towards his sister, but the talkative John rambled on, speaking in a free and easy way of the girls he had grown up with.

During the last year Floyd had ceased to talk to his sister about his girlfriends, and they seldom came to his home. In her presence his comrades talked continually of school; but if she was busy near she could hear them laughing and chatting in tones different from the ones they used when she was there. She had tried in every way she could to attract them to her home, for formerly they had come in great crowds. But Floyd did not seem to want them; he preferred going to their homes.

At times she wondered if she had been in their way when they had come.

When the two girls came she greeted them warmly; they had belonged to the crowd which had come in the past often for cookies and for help in long, knotty problems. Then, thinking they might not remain if she was present, she went into the next room. Through the open door she watched them. She could not help watching; she had been deprived of all her girlhood and now she wanted to enjoy theirs.

Dorothy, a dimpled, laughing girl with great, brown eyes and masses of curls which were always rumpled, threw her hat into a chair and was soon seated between the two boys, showing them the posters she had made for Floyd. The sister saw Floyd move very close to the girl and lay his hand on her shoulder with a caressing movement; she caught the glance that he gave— a glance full of bold admiration and meaning. Rose stood near the table, watching the other girl. In her eyes was a look of longing, and yet it was mingled with fear. The three on the sofa soon drew her into their circle, John was open in his admiration of both girls; he tried to distribute his caresses with an impartial hand, but the little Rose drew away with that expression of dread in her eyes. Floyd was not so bold; he lightly laid his hand on her hand, and when she did not resent it clasped it more firmly. Her face flushed, but she suffered the hand to remain.

Elizabeth was called from the room by some visitors. When they had finally gone she came back to her former seat. She saw a new brother, a different one from the one she knew. He was talking in a boisterous tone.

"When are you going to kiss me good-bye, Dot?" he asked.

"Right at the station," she answered laughingly.

"Honor bright?" He asked.

"Honor bright," she promised.

"You are all right," he exclaimed. "Rose is too bashful for that." Then he hinted, "But you see I am going to take her home tonight."

Rose colored as he gave her a significant look. She pushed his hand from her arm and walked to the piano. But there was a wavering, an uncertainty in her face. He had been her comrade so long and she really liked him.

The watching sister made a quick decision. When the girls rose to go, she stood up saying, "Floyd, I want you and John to watch the house. I have to see Rose's mother tonight; tomorrow you can see the girls again."

There came a flush of annoyance on the boyish face, followed by one of anger. He knew his sister had been listening. But he was still too loyal to criticize her to John, who, when they were alone, openly denounced her for her meddling.

* * * * *

When she returned Floyd was alone. He sat sulky and silent. She busied herself with the household cares for a few minutes. Soon she went over to the lounge and sat down beside him. She put her arm around him and kissed his forehead. "Let's don't be angry on our last night," she begged.

"Why did you do it?" he asked. "I know you heard what I said to Rose, but what is she to you?"

"A great deal," she responded, "but not so much as the boy I love so dearly—the boy I have been a mother to, and yet I haven't been a true mother, for I never have talked to you of these things because they were hard. You see I have failed in my duty."

Instantly he was all tenderness. He drew her down into his boyish long arms and laid his head against hers. "You have not failed in anything, you darling!" he cried. "But it wouldn't hurt me. I'm a man. All the fellows do that way."

"How do you know?"

"They tell about it. We don't all talk about it in a crowd, but just when we are together, like John and me."

"Does John treat Rose that way?"

The boy grew warm in a minute. "He'd better not; he went too far to suit me tonight."

"Why did he?" she asked quietly. "You were rather free towards Dorothy."

"Dorothy is different; she's a— she's—well, she's a jolly good fellow, but Rose—well, I like Rose, and every fellow better keep his hands off her. I don't want a girl all the fellows can love; but I'm different. Those things don't hurt a fellow; he's coarser and—well, it's expected of him."

"But they do hurt you," she said. "The little book of memories that Rose gave you this afternoon told a story of its own. I am going to tell you this story."

He looked away into the distance, and she began.

*   *   *   *   *

"Once there was a man who went into a garden. All around him were beautiful roses of all colors. But he chose a little white bud for his. He chose it because it was pure and white, but most of all because it was closed. No other person could see into its heart.

While he was waiting for it to unfold he walked around to enjoy the other flowers. He studied their coloring and he breathed their perfume. For a long time he enjoyed this; then he wanted to get nearer to these roses, to handle them. Other travellers were handling them and they seemed to enjoy themselves more than he did. So he touched one rather timidly; others he was not so careful with. At last he grew tired and wandered back to his own rosebud and lo! it had opened. It stood the whitest and most fragrant rose in the garden, and its heart was the dewiest and most tender. But he remembered the crimson roses and it seemed too white.

Then he could not detect its fragrance, for he had killed his sense of smell by its abuse with the other roses, some of which stood as high and beautiful as before, but others were left bruised and broken by his ruthless desire to please, yes, to indulge himself. As he plucked his own rose, he was aware of no sense of joy over it, except from pride, for many travellers cast him envious glances. But he could not see its unusual beauty; he could not get the fragrance from its heart, because his sense of sight had been dulled by the brilliancy of the other flowers and his sense of smell by their odor.

"Nor did he think of the little buds in the garden that he had touched and then left. They would perhaps open, but the petals he had touched would always be brown and torn. The passers-by might not see them when the flowers had opened and revealed their hearts, but the men who had plucked them would—not at once, but when they had become less entranced and were seeking for defects. Then perhaps they would throw the roses away. But the man who had the perfect rose—the one which was perfect because it had been well protected—did not know of the havoc he had wrought.

He was too much interested in wondering why he did not enjoy his rose, why it seemed so commonplace and really tiresome. He did not know that it was he who had become unable to appreciate it, through his own indulgence begun in an idle moment, while he had waited for his flower to blossom."

*   *   *   *   *

She paused to look into his face. He was listening. Then she went on:

"You say you are a man; you have only thought of one side; you have only wanted the perfect rose. You may get one, but if you do it will be one which has been carefully guarded. You are not intending to break or bruise the other roses; you are just going to handle them because the other boys do. You will enjoy their fragrance, but you will leave wounded petals. Then after a time, if you travel far enough into the garden, you will grow indifferent to the havoc you are doing and will carelessly crush the flowers. You may grow so cruel that you will enjoy it.

There are men who do, and they started out as free from intention to harm as you were tonight. You caressed Dorothy; John caressed her. The next boy who comes along will find it easier to be free with her, and unless there is someone who cares enough to guard her she will be torn from the stem before she has blossomed. If you had kissed Rose tonight it would have been easy for you to kiss her again. You haven't yet, have you?"

He shook his head.

"I am so glad," she continued. "It will be so much better for her. If she permits you these familiarities she will permit others the same ones. She may soon become as reckless as Dorothy, and then we dare not think of the future. You can see now what a wonderful flower she promises to make. She is a perfect little bud. Would you not hate to think that you were spoiling the promise of that bud?"

"Forgive me for being so cross," he begged.

"Yes, dear," and she kissed his forehead. "But we are going to look at your side now. God made you so that you have certain desires, certain cravings, that you are to control. Many men will say that they are only to be satisfied, but we know better. The first kiss you give to a girl thrills you—really it is one of the greatest minutes of your life. The next girl you kiss seems less of a pleasure. Then after a while it becomes a mere habit; it loses all sense of enjoyment—the holiness has long since been done away with. Stronger desires than kissing arise and soon you are not the man God intended you to be. You will have a low idea of women. Even your wife, if you get the sweetest and purest in the world, will not seem so to you. Marriage will not be a sacred fulfillment; it will be a commonplace event."

His arms had tightened around her, but he was silent.

"And," she continued, "your future career as a man will be touched. You cannot think clearly or act quickly when any of the senses of your body have been impaired. Lust kills ambition, ability and power. I do not mean that every boy who starts in this way has the same fatal ending, but a great many do. There is the half-way place where many men stop; yet you will find they are not real men. It will be so much holier and better to stay at the beginning."

She sat silent, waiting for him to speak. At last he did. "Of course, Beth, I wouldn't want to go even half-way, now; I wouldn't even want to touch"— and a tender smile played around his lips—"any roses but one. But I cannot see yet why I can't let her know that I care for her; I will be constant. I want to like her and I want her to like me."

She drew a sharp breath. "You mean you will crush the petals of your own rose, and then enjoy the heart when it is opened. When you come back you may not even want to see that heart; you are just a boy. If you do, there will be times when you will see those crushed petals and be sorry. You may blame yourself, but you will probably blame Rose. You may grow so discontented that you will blame another man. If you know she allowed you these caresses, these little familiarities, you will think she would allow others."

He spoke with pride. "I know Rose."

"We will look at it from her side. After she realizes those petals have been crushed by you she may be afraid of the future. She may be afraid that you have wandered far into the garden and come back to her a worn-out traveller. She may be afraid that you will not appreciate her and that you will not deal rightly with her."

He laughed. "I am not afraid of that."

"Other girls just as constant in their friendship as Rose have felt that way," she said in a low voice.

"What do you mean?" he asked.

"My dear boy, I have a few wilted petals and I know how they feel. You see, I was like you are. There was no one to guard me and I did just what any girl will do who does not think. But I realized in time to save myself from only a few brown ones, and I want to save every girl I can. We were young and thought we knew our hearts. My, how they changed! But they couldn't change those bruised petals."

He gave a hurt cry, but he saw a face free from suffering. It held only love for him.

"Floyd, I want to give the world a noble man. That is the dearest wish of every woman. I want to give some woman a pure husband; and oh, my darling boy, I want to give you life in its best and purest forms. I put the first little garment on your little body; I changed you from a little angel to a human being, and I must care for that human being."

"You angel!" he murmured.

She lifted his chin and looked into his clear eyes.

"I promise," he said in a low tone.

"It will not be easy, dear. You will have to refuse to listen to other boys, you will have to read only good books and you will have to think pure thoughts.

Rose's little book will help you. You can see the baby that I am trying to keep pure and help me do it; you can see those doll shoes and remember how you suffered on the night you wanted to be happy, because you wanted to do as 'the fellows' did. You were so anxious to know what was in the heart of the rose book. I do not know, but she did tell me this. On the second petal—and you must look at it every day—is the little picture of Sir Galahad which your first teacher gave you. Do you remember it?"

The boy smiled dreamily as he quoted—

My strength is as the strength of ten,

Because my heart is pure.

34

CPSIA information can be obtained at www.ICGtesting.com
Printed in the USA
BVOW03s2211281014

372766BV00024B/314/P